Under a Kindred Moon

Jo Lynn Stresing

For Kindred Spirit Kitty —
Fantastic to workshop with
you fellow writer !

XXOO Jo Lynn

ISBN-13:
978-1546852773

ISBN-10:
1546852778

Editor, Linda Lowen
Cover & Book Design, Kay Stresing

For Kevin

With special thanks to:
Editor Linda Lowen
Graphic Designer Kay Stresing
Dr. Frank Capella, DVM
Siberian Husky family and friends

Under a Kindred Moon

Winter's Dream

Snow swirling silent

at dawn I rise

from a pine shelter

clutching my fleece,

crunching fresh trail,

to a waiting dog yard.

Spinning chains ring,

furred faces spring

from straw singing

for the master

a new day.

Leather gloves traded,

feed donated,

no rhyme, no reason

or justification.

Just love an adventure,

life purpose, surrender,

to a dream, of dogs, of sled.

Full Bloom Day

Not everyone had a white picket fence, but it was definitely suburbia. Each yard, an eighth-acre lot, side by side, back to back, pressed together between perfect tree-lined streets. Where home repairs, lawn mowing and floor waxing were on schedule, storm windows and summer screens exchanged every spring and fall, indoor and outdoor house painting and holiday decorating done by calendar date. Each house mirrored another, one weed-free lawn flowing into the next, the symmetry, the order, the constant watchful eye. No one decided to have a neighborhood watch, there just was one. Nosy neighbors tattling on each others' kids was the tasty fat of the day. *Your cats are scratching in my garden again. The neighbor kids were playing on our deck when we weren't home. They picked flowers that didn't belong to them. Your son peeped into our daughter's window and your dandelions are seeding our lawn, again,* and on and on for years. Friday night was for daddy's homemade fudge, Sunday was for church and family dinner.

Since Mamma was a farm girl at heart, I was allowed the occasional distraction of rescuing an injured bird, turtle, or frog, or an assortment of caterpillars in jars, but that was the extent of it. So at the time of my tenth birthday, it was a revelation, a radical, truly original idea, a soul-sought rescue mission for a lonely daughter flying in the face of father disapproval, that in a large cardboard box would be a real puppy dog. A breath of air in the suffocating order, a shedding, pooping, pissing, howling puppy with winter white fur and chocolate kissing eyes. Sure there was talk of responsibility, of feeding and training, of poop duty and extra yard mowing and a whole new set of rules, but it turned out, in time, the parents were head over heels for her too and trained her impeccably well. I had heard that dogs had exceptional hearing and I experimented with calling her at a parental inaudible whisper into my bed at night. She would cuddle warmly at my cold feet until my mom would discover and scold her at the last nightly patrol before they would turn in. Daddy even jogged with her off lead in the neighborhood and he had total instant recall, commanding her "come over" to heel left position and "go out, go" to release. She had shined to his harsh talk and punishing corrections much better than me, becoming a pleasure to take out walking in the neighborhood.

One hundred sixty homes occupied eight rows of residential streets framed by the parallel avenues of South Bay and Saint Marks. From the main street Town Hall, South Bay Avenue became the gravel road to the town beach, and Saint Marks ended at a private road after crossing Maple Street. South of Maple were hundreds of acres of undeveloped woods that sat between suburbia and the Long Island Sound.

My puppy dog, who my father named Penuche for her vanilla fudge color, was the perfect companion to explore the world. We would escape the neighborhood by cutting through certain backyards and walking many blocks until we came to the dirt mouth of the private road. Then we would slip into the woods on a kid-carved path that would lead to the edge of the first estate. The dark, dense woods would open into a mowed grass field with an apple orchard, glass greenhouse, rose garden with a sundial pedestal and rock patio with a large Victorian mansion in the distance. The outlying greenhouse was the closest I dared go to be assured I would not be discovered by the owners. Fresh signs were hanging for the upcoming horticulture society's rose competition. From behind the greenhouse I hugged the tree line for camouflage and could cross the length of the field to a proper trail. In the spring it was lined with clusters of the most exotic, extraordinary daffodils, varieties I had never seen before or since. Penuche would run and explore, circling about me, never leaving sight of me, able to be recalled to my side at a moment's notice if either of us were getting into danger or trouble. The perfect sidekick, courage on four legs.

Trespassing those woods was a whole day's plan. I'd pack a lunch, leave after breakfast and be home just before dinner. At night when I lay my head down, I'd see the woods rushing by my closed eyes in an unsummoned review of the day. The trail was long and deep, taking hours, and if I persisted would eventually come to a large clear-running stream, perfect for my dog to wade or drink. Water plants floated along or were attached and bobbed in the bubbling current. Carp and goldfish flashed orange as I picked large blackberries overhanging the water in thick juicy clumps that stained my fingers as I grabbed them. Sometimes I would pick to take home, but mostly I'd eat my fill on the spot. One time, I followed the stream for what seemed like miles until it came to a 12-foot chain link fence that just let the water run under it. Nothing else could pass. When I saw the electric wire lining the top I quickly called and clipped the dog to a pocketed leash I had with me. The thick woods and pricker bushes pressed against the fence blocking the view everywhere but where the stream entered. From the water the view was where Cinderella must meet Beauty and the Beast. The stream led to a very large pond crowded with ducks and geese, some with exotic plumed feathered headdresses and fancy wings and tail feathers, giant white fairytale geese, purple and green-crested mallards, diving mergansers, spotted loons, and all other manner of unusually pattered fowl. Then I saw them, a pair of black swans with dark orange beaks, gliding together in perfect unison, their necks each forming half the shape of a heart as they crossed the open water in front of a rose-lined stone pathway leading to a green and white-awned castle just beyond. I was astounded by the view.

It was at my second spying that I heard him yell, "This is private property." My heart pounded and I ran as fast as I could, the leashed dog pulling me. When I stopped to catch my breath, even though I was most of the long way out, I caught a glimpse of a trim gentleman still striding behind me. Silver haired, but not too old in dress slacks and a v-neck sweater, he could have been Jay Gatsby himself. Ahead of me a strong white dog in the lead. Breathless I whispered, "Good girl. Go out, go."

Nationals

The walkway lined with retired sleeper cars are reserved for the most affluent guests. The rose gardens are in full bloom among the abundant fountains and koi ponds. The leaves here have not yet turned. I try to breath in the loveliness of each day knowing that back home the bitter soaking rain has already ripped and pelted all the colored maple leaves from the trees and they are clumped in soggy wet piles everywhere unprotected by kennel roofs.

The Chattanooga Choo Choo Hotel is strewn this week with show dog exhibitors exercising well-furred and quaffed specimens at every waking hour. In front of traditional hotel rooms in buildings two and three, the sprawling parking lot is littered with dog show vans. Shiny new vehicles, with airbrushed kennel logos and reflective shade tarps, are the perfect facade for resentful spouses, abandoned bosses, strained dog-care helpers, credit card debt and the exhaustion of the exhibitors.

At each dawn the grounds come alive with owners in sweatpants or pajamas beginning the day's endless walking of dogs. These perfect dog specimens they're sure will be declared best are howling from various vehicles throughout the parking lot waiting for the first morning's outing. They call and answer to other vans as dogs are leashed and sprung by their owners. Some folks are riding golf carts or bicycles with their tethered friend trotting beside, but most are leash walking one or two at a time. The dogs are trained against their natural sled dog pulling nature to accommodate their human owners who are dragged by the most exuberant specimens.

At the other end of the parking lot are the concrete renters. Three rows of serious motor home dog show living. Grandeur on wheels, homes away from home, they are tightly parked with fancy awnings, strings of lights, jack o' lanterns, lawn chairs, and barbecues. Exercise pens are set up in between each, with plastic oriental-patterned rugs beneath, designed to keep the dogs coats clean. Car reserving cones and extension cords popping neon color are running everywhere. Generators and air conditioners hum in the temporary neighborhood speckled with many distant license plates. Many have come a long way for this annual Siberian Husky National Specialty extravaganza.

The National Specialty this year is an Indian summer vacation for me and many others from colder Northern states. Freezing rain and first snow are dusting my kennel by now just in time for Halloween. I am relieved not to see our few pathetic trick-or-treaters showing up in costumes half-obliterated by winter coats and snow suits. Snow and slush will add another layer to the trudge of dog chores waiting for me when I get home. My huskies are an exuberant athletic group. Every fall they are wilder and louder than usual when excited by the coming snow and cold. Leaping and bounding, pacing feet pounding on fencing, they will be anxiously vocal about their needs to be exercised, watered and fed. Protective work gloves, boots and a hooded suit will be part of my daily uniform soon.

At the specialty in Tennessee, we are wearing tee shirts, sneakers and summer dress skirts and suits. In addition to the all-day dog showing, the week is crammed with socials, club meetings, banquets, fundraisers and seminars, most for the financial benefit of the host parent club. There is a rescue parade one afternoon to honor owners who have adopted and trained unwanted dogs. Some events are silly in nature, like an after-hours show dog costume contest. Still others, like an invitational parade of the top 20 Siberian Huskies in the country or an awards banquet, are formalwear red-carpet evening events. Some guest speakers lecture about certain aspects of the breed such as genetics, early Siberian history, or specific dog care.

Standing at the back of one of the free seminars, the reserved seats in front of me are mostly taken by newer members and owners trying to learn about Siberian Huskies. The spectating students rustle their questionnaires. They are to be student judges of the six dogs being presented in the show ring in front of them. It's not well attended by the general membership even though it is conducted by the honorary lifetime members and judges involved in the breed and dog sledding for decades. Some are Iditarod and Yukon Quest participants, knowing hundreds of grueling arctic miles, having been in the breed long enough to have met some of the breed's founding fathers. Old eyes that saw early heroic dogs and studied with the great Siberian Husky masters.

The premise is simple. Six Siberians are presented in a mock show ring, each with a handler who is not their owner. That way the usual show ring politics are eliminated if one knows who is the owner or breeder of the dog. The spectators are asked to judge each dog from best to worst on separate aspects considered important to this breed including movement, proportion, substance, structure, form, function, type, head and coat. The mentor will then do the same, explaining why they judged the way they did.

To present proper gait each of the six dogs are gaited several times. Towards and away to display front and rear movement and a moving profile to view side gate.

The two dogs determined best moving by the elder judges are plain gray, brown-eyed bitches. Refined, fast, they float effortlessly beside the handlers with plenty of daylight under their slim chests. Later I learn they are litter sisters who run as partners sledding all winter with their owner. The next, placed third, is a handsome red male trotting distinctly and covering a lot of ground, his four legs landing squarely under him. A bit *beefcake* it is how it is described, but strong and determined. Two other males judged forth and fifth seem bouncy and a little silly, but have some speed and pace to be admired.

The seated students gasp and moan as the last place is assigned to a velvet-gleaming jet black coated, blue-eye bitch. Folks can't take their eyes off her, but it is explained, the dog lumbers too long bodied for the breed's original function. These working dogs are quick and light on their feet, able to perform their original function in harness most capably, carrying a light load at a moderate speed over great distances.

I overhear the short blond in front of me. Her student judging did not match that of the old pros.

"Why would they put a beautiful dog like that in last place?"

"Who cares about sled movement and their original sledding function?"

"Who needs sled dogs? We live in a modern society don't we?"

Her friend nods. She agrees."It is a dog SHOW."

"That black one should be at the front of the line. So pretty. She looks a lot like my new puppy Maggie Pie... doesn't she?"

In all but the final category, this beauty is determined the last placement giving her an overall score of fourth or fifth. In the final judged section of type, head, and coat, she is finally moved to the front of the line, placed first, much to the relief of the shaken newcomers.

Giving Thanks for a Canine Day

The soup, the slump, the gizzards, the rump,

the paper sack within.

The neck, the heart, the giblets, the art

of crispy, crackling skin.

The broth, the drippings, the fat and liver,

The juices must run a clear river.

The bones, the trimmings, the slivers, the scraps

the grease, the tail and turkey backs.

The wings, the drumsticks, the thighs,

and carved white breasts.

Light meat or dark

Which do you request?

I knew darn well the turkey was the only thing I had in common with

other Thanksgiving traditions. I had been doing it my way for so

long I didn't think much about it. I knew there were 6 am risings in

other houses to get the big birds stuffed and dressed and into the

ovens for midday feasts, cloth table settings, pie bakings, and silver polishings. The planning and perfectness would go on for days. The supply must be ready for the soon-to-be overstuffed football snoozers. Maybe wine would be poured while the turkey sat for 20 minutes before an official carving. Maybe grace would be said. Would there be fancy cut glass pickle and cranberry trays, or green bean casseroles reserved for only this occasion? Some kind of probably mashed potatoes, and stuffing and there must be gravy. I had grown up in this same way.

But in my house today the thawed turkey would be roasted to a safe 160 degrees. Whole unpeeled potatoes, and cut up squash might accompany it. When the turkey was deemed done, the choicest meat, some breast and maybe a drumstick would be designated for human consumption. The rest would be gathered together in a large stock pot; the giblets including heart, liver, gizzards and neck, the skin, the fat, all scraps and trimmings, the bones, the fatty tail with its few pin feathers, and all the pan drippings. All the parts, spare and otherwise, would become a turkey soup, a cooked up slump. Next, the bare bones after being boiled clean, would be meticulously picked leaving a meaty, hearty, chunky, fatty broth to be ladled in stainless steel dishes over dry kibble on a cold November night. Oh happy dogs, Thanksgiving dinner is served!

Meet the Breed

Set off in spontaneous unison, the ancient voices of our arctic tribe sound to announce feeding time, the arrival or departure of strangers, the occasional full moon or the birth or death of one of our own Siberian Husky pack. At other times, there is some mystery: why a group serenade now? A lone dog's howl begins it and others join in; a song for song's sake is all I can determine. The demonic volume or dissonant pitch is not frightening if you know them.

The kennel is an unmistakable pack of elders, adults and puppies. Working class sled dogs in family groups with upright ears and coarse but soft fur in copper or light reds, grays or blacks, all trimmed in white face and feet. Their expressive brush tails can joke or boss, warn or invite.

In this pen there are shades of red and white, a mother and two daughters and a foolish younger half brother who can run like the wind with his taut straight back, and keeps things stirred up with his restless antics. His curved sickle tail touches his back ready to spring into a wag or a pounce. He is the talker of this group and is often hushed for vocalizing when spectators visit. The girls in the pen adore him and take turns managing and scolding his exuberance with gentle bites to his neck and face. His mom seems satisfied with her daughters taking on this task, leaving her in peaceful observance.

They flash with blue or amber eyes and gleaming fur, active in the mornings and evenings, lounging on top of their well-worn wooden houses, touching back to back or shoulder to shoulder, with a head or paw draped over another's back or neck. They are a family.

Another pen is a group of three grays and one dark black bitch with a widow's peak pointing down deeply between her piercing obsidian eyes. Her heart-shaped Elizabethan collar of dark fur frames her open white face. We have named her 'Jewel' for obvious reasons. Two of the grays she lives with are her sister and mother who are both bi-eyed, both having the blue eye on the left. The mom is shedding very late this year and has patches of old tufting fur decorating her hind quarters in contrast with the shining new coat that is growing in.

The third gray in this pen is a big male called 'River', short for "Kindred Moon's River Dance". He is blue-eyed, handsome and athletic. He flirts shamelessly with both teenage girls, keeping his future breeding options well greased. He leads the charge when it is their turn to run into the big play yard while their pen is being cleaned. The mom and yearling girls take cheap shots biting each other once one of them is the designated rabbit of their chase game.

Another pen has three six month old sibling puppies, each more beautiful than the next. The gray and white girl favors her mom but with a full dark wide stripe between her eyes from her forehead all the way down to her jet black nose. She was a very fast running puppy named 'Mariah' as in "they call the wind." Her sister is a dilute black, less leggy and with a shorter neck, but the perfect planed head and one striking watch eye with a blue and brown iris resembling the pattern of the Chinese ying and yang symbol. Their brother is a furry jet black showy male with a Zorro mask.

He is named "man in black" with the nickname of 'Cash'. He is always a good sport with a calm easygoing attitude when his sisters outwrestle or outrun him. With their mother and father penned in close watchful proximity, the pups are free to test their agility, cunning, and craftiness with each other. These youngsters are bright and shiny with new untarnished fur and gleaming white teeth. They are funny, curious and demanding little troublemakers that I could not part with.

Two other pens are a whole litter of seven whites who are my team. Their mother was a white born to us from two grays each with only one white in their pedigree six generations back. The litter is housed in side-by-side living quarters. Two big silly boys and two smaller and very affectionate girls occupy the corner pen. The siblings beside them are a slicker, faster boy and two larger females almost his size. They are the real speed and smarts of the group and are my leaders.

Mother 'Dori', a flawless lead dog, now almost 11 years old, was a natural born sled dog who taught her sons and daughters the gee and haw, right and left of it. Together as a group we are not always the fastest team on the circuit but can place an honest second or third with much less training than we should have had. We look flashy on the trail, resembling photos from the 1930s when white Siberian Huskies were in fashion.

There are 22 pens in all, each with a more beautiful gathering than the group before. "Animal hoarder, crazy dog women. How many do you have now dear?" had swum in my head from time to time. But the matriarch and patriarchs with their tattered, thick old coats gather together and whisper to the dog gods and exchange knowing glances. No white picket fences for her. She has provided. We have birthed in her bed, we have taken her sleep. In the mud and the rain and the brutal snow, in the red and green of new life, and the purging and cleaning of the old and dying ones, she has kept us safe, dry, fed, and together. We have lived the life of real dogs. We have known the belonging. We have run the forest trails in the wind and the falling snow in our family groups with only the swish of the wooden runners behind us and her steady voice, "Good dogs, hike, hike."

Under a Kindred Moon

The full moon above makes the dog yard daylight bright. Thick carpet grass is covered by a thin layer of icy snow. Bounding silhouettes of the breeding pair dart back and forth to all areas of the fenced yard. Her shape shows more white leg and face than his dark coat and mask against the blackened pines.

My husband and I stand quietly. The hard snow crunches under our feet when we move. The dogs run by to check in but do not stop to see us. They prefer to flag, flirt and mount a private distance away. If we interact with them they are distracted from the task we are requesting they perform. It is 13 degrees. We started several hours ago. Near midnight now, I am booted and snow-suited with a down coat, hat, overhood and ear band pulled over my nose and mouth. My husband let me wear his warmest lined leather gloves. I fear I'll get cold with the wait.

This is our third night attempt. The dogs have been flirting but not yet mating. Each night the chosen husky pair look forward to the extra let out for an evening arctic romp. There is only a few day window for breeding success. Tonight the male is mounting her frequently. She is signaling him by flagging her tail to her side encouraging his advances. She stands solid and tilts her pelvis towards him when he attempts. From my post of thirty feet away I see her head bow low with his push and his back feet lift ever so slightly off the ground.

"That looks good," my husband whispers

"Don't rush it, wait... wait."

Lola lets out a low pain moan. Max stands connected at the hips. They are tied. We begin our approach carefully so as not to disconnect their attachment, spook them loose. My husband reaches her collar first. I'm two seconds behind to catch the male's thick neck. We are the place keepers now holding them so no one gets injured in the 20 to 40 minute lock up. The dogs are friendly to us as the four of us huddle together. They are comforted by our guidance and presence.

My job is to hold the male as this is the easier task. He is warm. I dig one hand into his soft fur under his collar. He must stand still until her body releases him. Some males will be impatient and fidgety, try to run off and end up dragging her. If he struggles or pulls he may hurt her or permanently injure himself. I am ready with all of my strength to control him if I need to, but Max is patient to stand. He is tail-wagging happy and licks my face. He enjoys the special praise and attention.

Two brief moments are uncomfortable for Lola and she whines and writhes impatient with the tight connection, but mostly her eyes are glossy with a look of hazy contentment. She wags her tail and lays her chest in my husband's lap for support. He pets her and says "good girl" in his deep soothing voice. All of us tire of the confinement. My knees and back are stiff and begin to tremble. I shift my weight, careful not to disturb. If I kneel it is easier on my back but I have less leverage if he struggles against my hold, so I stand bent initially and then drop to one knee partway through.

After about 30 minutes the dogs both look down in surprise. He has softened enough to be released. We have pre-clipped leashes to each collar to walk the dogs back to their separate quarters. As sperm live for several days the pair does not need to mate again for 48 hours. We are tired and cold. It is late and we have to get up early in the morning. I can rest easy tonight with the hope waiting families will get pups they are requesting. That another generation is in the making.

Blackbird Fly

Raven likes the soft pillows, six against the headboard. She pants hotly into my ear off and on through the night. The inevitable event is several days away I think. She's too calm to start tonight, but every female has her own style of labor. I note she is not displaying classic signs of frequent panting, pawing, digging, or personal licking and looking. The closer to the birth she comes, even if it's her first time, she will instinctively know and show that something is happening that night.

This will be Raven's first litter. She is a calm, sensible black and white that seems unflappable in all training and sledding experiences so far, but I have no way of knowing how her birthing might progress. Hormones, anatomy, and the number of puppies conceived will all influence the progression and outcome. For my part as assistant and midwife, the most crucial thing is not to miss any distress signs including green or red discharge prior to first puppy born and to know when the water breaks.

The water breaking is the start of the birth clock. A puppy needs to be born within an hour or two of that event. If I miss the breaking water, which can happen if I am not looking at her, I will not know when to start timing. I might find a puddle after the fact, but typically the pregnant female will lick up all the evidence immediately. Lest we forget our dogs are animals, in the wild the protection of a litter is based in part on it remaining undetected by possible predators. Elimination of all body fluids that emit odors is the best way to ensure the secret location of the den.

In this case, Raven's special hiding place is among the pillows of my bed. The first couple of nights I invited her into the bedroom, she was up and down all night jumping on and off the bed, snooping joyfully around the room. Raven enjoyed the freedom of being out of her downstairs crate, playing with dog toys and chews from the bedroom stash, thereby keeping me awake most of the night. By the third evening she had settled into the bed, deciding the bedroom was indeed suitable and, most especially, the pillows were the perfect nest.

I'd typically invite my pregnant bitches upstairs overnight about a week prior to their due date, so that by the time they are ready to birth, they understood where, and are familiarized with my human surroundings. While assisting my first dog with her first litter, I moved downstairs to a makeshift doggie birthing room to supervise, attempting to keep my own bedroom pristine.

After the first sleepless event I decided it wasn't very comfortable for either of us. I learned if the dog came upstairs instead, she had special human time in the best den of the house, and I was able to sleep in between the nesting in my usual comfort. It was easier to know when the water broke if I was in the same room or, better yet, in the same bed as my furry, four legged birth partner.

Each bitch's water breaking is a little different. Some startle with a big sudden gush that takes me and the dog by surprise, but usually a few small drops will leak in advance, sometimes with a bit of the softened stringy membrane. Once you have touched the actual birth water it is unmistakable from that day forward. It has a slippery, silky quality, a touch like that of bleach water, and should be clear colored prior to the first puppy being born.

Every birthing female has her own contraction style too. Some lavishly stretch with legs fully extended behind, some progress in shorter leg pushing strokes bunny hop style, some have visible abdominal crunches, muscles clutching as the puppy moves into the birth canal. A pup is about to be born when a low squeeze gut grip lifts the fox brush tail. The more prominently the tail lifts, the nearer the puppy is to its exit from the mother's birth canal.

It is mid-morning the next day and I am finished feeding, watering and scooping the poop of all my other dogs. It takes several hours every morning. This day, since the puppies were not born last night, I speed through everyone's care, anxious to get back to the bedroom to check on Raven. As I settle in beside her I notice a few drops of clear fluid. She is licking herself vigorously and the underside of her tail is a bit wet. I'm relieved the rest of the kennel is set for their day as Raven begins some real stretching contractions on her bed nest of pillows. Several moments later she's up to rotate her position and partially squats with a sac showing. Then the sac squirted open, a typical water breaking prior to the first puppy presenting that starts the birth clock.

Raven's panting remains pretty constant. After her water breaks I anxiously long for the safe birth of the first puppy. It could be born live and die in the first few moments fighting for its first breath. It could be born dead, or not be born at all and require rushing to the vet for an emergency C-section. Usually if the first puppy is born live, the rest of the litter has a good chance of being born live too. Waiting and praying for Raven and mother nature was all that could be done this early on.

She showed many good strong contractions and tail lifting but still no puppy sac presented. Then I saw it. A small, pointed protrusion from the soft rose shape swelling under her tail. On the next push, I saw it again, pointed white, like the tip of a watercolor paint brush. The next contraction poking out just a little further, I saw the black banded tail of a black and white puppy and beside it two small paws. Breach! Not the worst thing, but with its fur growing in the opposite direction of the birth, it makes the puppy surprisingly harder to push out, especially for the first one venturing out of the virgin birth canal. After several more sharp pushes with the puppy not changing its position, I gently guided feet and tail out towards me. My vet always says, "Grab two of something", meaning a tail and foot or two feet would be safe, just a tail or one foot, not. Within several seconds the whole sac was out.

Grab a birth towel.

Clear sac and fluids away from the face.

Peel back the sack to find the umbilical cord.

Clamp the cord near the pup.

A few inches from the first clamp

second hemostat clamps the afterbirth.

Non-sharp baby scissors in between,

don't cut puppy feet, only cut the cord

in between the two hemostats.

Gently pull the afterbirth out.

Give the afterbirth to Raven.

It's okay if she eats it as nature intended.

Now, vigorously dry her puppy while swinging its lungs clear.

Protect its head and neck from whiplash.

Pinch back of puppy neck to produce crying if it's not.

Continue vigorous towel drying, while you tie off the cord.

Dental floss is preferred, but not flavored. Don't give Raven

any reason to chew or lick at it for the 24-36 hours it takes to

dry and then fall off, otherwise the pup could bleed out.

I tie off the cord as quickly as I can. This time my hands are shaking badly and the puppy is wriggling active. I give it back to its mom who has been licking up fluids and eating the nutrient-rich afterbirth. By now Raven is more than ready to greet her new dog. A little black and white boy. She licks him completely claiming him as her own. Her scented saliva unmistakably marks that he is her son.

I know we must successfully repeat this process six more times. At the veterinarian's usual instruction, 55 days from the mating, Raven had an x-ray to count the number of puppies in the litter. This practice seems unnatural to me, but is the ultimate way to keep puppies and mother safe. As the birth progresses, knowing how many puppies remain is crucial to any emergency decision-making. A palpation and general checkup confirmed the pregnancy at 29 days, but was not an actual head count. In Raven's case at least four puppies were determined at this early date. The recent x-ray totaled the puppy count at seven. This is a big litter for any Siberian Husky. The breed, being of arctic origins, typically has only four to six.

Living the moment of each puppy birth, step by step as it presents, is the only way to be there for Raven. It involves meticulously tending to each sac, each cord, each breath and getting each pup's first nursing accomplished, all the while recording time for the crucial knowledge of how long in between each birth. As I am waiting on number four, I'm relieved we are halfway there almost. I am watching the clock, 30 minutes, 45 minutes, one hour, reminding myself that is still "okay" between pups. As long as she is not straining. If she is resting or working on having the next, resting between is okay. An hour between is typical, but two hours is still okay. Don't panic, all is still well.

While waiting, I am on-the-spot bargaining with my faith of convenience, praying to the dog gods, to Raven's fateful angels and anywhere else I can. I am no longer wishing for the colors or sexes of the pups. I am no longer concerned if my six-generational plan of finally having a whole black and white litter might come to fruition. "Please let it be a normal home birth. Please let all of them make it out ALIVE." Please don't let anything happen to my beloved Raven.

I know firsthand that if too much time passes between pups and nothing is progressing then I will make the inevitable call to the vet. Then I'll be on their clock. I will follow the call with the probable emergency visit, sometimes birth assistance, but often a C-section that could mean life lost for the mother or puppies, not to mention the $1200 - $1500 surgery bill and the dreaded aftercare. If the mother can't perform, the puppies must be fed every two hours round the clock until she recovers or until they are three weeks old and able to eat on their own. The actual feeding is a daunting task. They can choke, aspirate, refuse the bottle, dehydrate, or not digest the man-made or other mammal formulas. By the time the last puppy is fed, two hours have nearly passed and it's time to start feeding the first puppy again. Some of the strong puppies might survive against insurmountable odds, but others will wail tiny ghostly inconsolable cries for hours prior to their desperately unavoidable heartbreaking deaths.

Hallucinations are a likely part of the round-the-clock days and nights of new born feedings. Maybe it's part of the stamina required for the breed. Many mushers have described sleep deprivation as being one of the many challenges of dog sledding at the Iditarod and other long distance races. At a sledding seminar a fellow musher explained it in terms of the impossible task of trying to buckle a watchband on his wrist. After trying and failing again and again for more than 30 minutes he eventually had to admit it was due to lack of sleep and moved on to something else. Another well-known driver thought she was mushing in a Candy Land board game with the dog team. She had to tell herself if it can't be real then it isn't. The most dangerous hallucination story I heard was about a musher who thought he saw a hotel, parked the dog team, rented a room and checked in for the night. Luckily a fellow musher thought it strange when he came upon the driverless team in the middle of the trail, on a night that was twenty degrees below zero. When he look around, he discovered the musher sleeping soundly in a nearby snow bank, woke him promptly and thereby saved his life.

  I have experienced hallucinations before with the occasional traumatic birth. For me, the waking dreams usually come as lost loved ones standing just out of peripheral vision, helplessly watching me struggle. When I turn to look directly at them to plea for assistance, they are gone. I embrace these mildly exhausted angel guides as harmless. I prefer them to my more severely exhausted forms, which roll from my mind and out my feet like so many lost marbles, sleep deprived creatures, phantom rats that scurry, running blackness into the darkened corners of the room.

But none of this for Raven. Each 45 minutes to an hour she would roust from the deep rest and contract deeply, effectively, several times. "Good girl. Yes, good girl" encouragement from me would greet each effort of labor. By puppy number five's birth, all black and white boys, I know I am home free with the wind at my back. I can almost will the last out with an oxytocin injection and some special prayers. If an hour or two pass and I know that only one pup is unborn, then it is safe for me to give an inter muscle injection at the midsection to produce the last few contractions. I have seen it work miraculously, but this time all Raven's pups are born before any intervention is necessary. The second to last is a black and white girl. At 45 minutes after number six, number seven, another girl presents and a few sharp pushes later and we are golden, a successful home birth. Seven black and whites. Every puppy and afterbirth accounted for. They are vigorous and ravenous as is Raven. They belly up to their nipple bar and latch on for their lives. Raven sleeps in between licking and nosing them. No stress, no trauma, no green distress discharge of puppies left too long, no lifeless puppies born too late. No strawberry milk of C-section blood mixing into cut milk ducts. They are born. They are here. They are safe.

So begins the battle of protecting umbilical cords from overzealous mother licks, the watchful deliberate warm wet cotton ball pooping and peeing of the puppies until the mom fully takes over cleaning them. So begins the labor of home cooking, feeding and brothing Raven so lots of milk is produced, the daily weigh ins and charting growth of each pup. The struggle of keeping the pups clean and safe with all other dog germs at bay. Not to mention keeping the newborns very warm. A chilled puppy cannot properly digest milk. They are neonates and cannot regulate their own body temperatures for several weeks.

So begins the battle fought for life, at first by the minute, then the hour, then day by day, for weeks, months and then years. So begins the seven headcount blackness, like a squirming pile of soft tent caterpillars trimmed with white face and feet. My seven in a row, jet black and gleaming new fur against the naked belly of Raven, with their perfect outlined ears and masked snouts. Lined-up heads are bobbing, suckling pumps, open-mouthed tongues cupping teats, the essence of Siberian Husky as pure and profound as I will ever see. Small new dogs with irrepressible, enthusiastic vigor, bound to them every future day of their lives. The perfect seven. The lucky seven. The living seven.

Like Clockwork

4:45 AM

Even in my absence I am right there with them, like twin speak, like soul mates. My clock is synchronized. I know their song of first light. I feel their pang, the calling of a new day. I hear the buzz of the alarm in our dark bedroom. I know he will hit the snooze. The current mamma will jump on the bed. He will pat and cuddle her for a brief reprieve. Although I'm not there, I picture him then, rising, with a stiff back, an old back. I know by this time he is rousting, stretching, reaching for her collar. I imagine him leashing her, then walking her, starting the day. A day in my absence. He is caring for my beloveds. Caring for my dogs.

5:00 AM

The light switch is flipped at the top of the worn wooden stair case, still without the handrail he never has time to put up. The mamma dog scurries down ahead of him. The pups are wildly vocalizing as soon as they hear his footsteps. Mamma automatically goes into the empty crate for the offered biscuit. She has no concern for her crying puppies. They are older now and she knows the routine.

5:15 AM

When Mamma is secured, the puppy room door is unlatched, swung open. An iron half-height grill still retains them. They are on hind legs, bellowing, wailing. It is feeding time. He is setting up food in four bowls now. Dry kernels, a quarter cup in each. They are beyond the nursing, beyond the baby rice evaporated milk weaning formula. Mamma dog scolded them away from her teats weeks ago. The pups have graduated from ground soaked starter food. They are rapidly growing, needing, springing and bounding. They are one week from the inevitable day of departure, leaving us to arrive as a new puppy at a waiting new home.

5:30 AM

The pups must be fed individually now to ensure that they all get the required amount. To accomplish this, a 4'x 8' birth box is set just outside the puppy room. It has been divided by four large uncovered plastic storage containers. One bowl of food is placed in each. He lifts and sets each puppy down into a box with its food. The puppy dives in and devours. We agreed he'd feed the four white pups first, each separately. They all look so much alike we devised this plan so no one gets skipped or fed twice. This also prevents a bigger pup from pushing a smaller pup aside as they did in their younger communal eating.

5:45 AM

When all four whites have eaten separately, simultaneously, they are each lifted back into the room. Three more bowls are filled now for the three reds, then two more for the two grays. When all nine are fed and returned back to the room, my patient husband steps over the baby gate and into their puppy room. Now that they have all eaten, they are calm. He scoops up one, then the next, until they all have had a cuddle with him. They each press flat bellied to his chest, bury their furry face into his beard, licking and snuggling, his big hands rubbing, stroking, and ruffing. Each pup waits for a turn. They chew on his puppy room slippers. He scuffs around, cooing at them, directing them, while folding and picking up puppy-soiled newspaper. A plastic bag lined can is just outside the room. He is compacting soggy paper in the can as he goes. He knows he will be slinging the big heavy bag to the dump in a few more days.

6:00 AM

Newspaper is gathered and stored in white-lidded buckets just outside the room but within reach. He brings newspaper home gathered from coworkers at his day job. He worries that he will run out, if he will have enough for the many changes of paper in a day. Reaching over the baby gate, he is grabbing three or four slightly read Sunday standards and some local market circulars. Now he is stooped, spreading them in the room, piece by piece until a large area is well covered. Pups are trotting, sniffing and admiring the new newspaper. Some are circling on the clean arrangement. Some will poop right then as it is freshly laid. Then it will need to be removed again, discarded and new sheets will be laid fresh, leaving plenty for the long day ahead.

6:15 AM

The pan of water still needs attention. The old water is dumped into a carefully placed bucket just within arm's reach. Pre-filled blue and white thermoses of water are dumped into the now empty pan. The pups charge in to drink, called by the sound of the chugging water. This is the only action this picnicware will ever know. The empty thermoses are set outside the room on a work counter. They will need to be refilled for the repeat midday feeding and cleaning. A urine-soaked pile of fake lamb-like sleeping blankets is the last attention to detail. He scoops them up and drops them into a waiting empty laundry basket. It's time for him to climb out of the room now. The pups face his exit at rapt attention, right against the baby barrier, as he drops clean puppy blankets into their sleeping corner. The room is all set. Just before departing to go to his real day job, the crate is opened for the observing mamma dog. Now anxious to see her babies, she easily leaps the gate clearing it and all pups as well. Her landing hardly dissuades the pups from their self placement at the barrier. They know their human is about to scoop a small handful of food and toss it into the room to lure them away from the gate. It is the only safe way to shut the door and avoid pinching small noses, paws or tails.

6:30 AM

They dart into the room, falling for the food distraction every time. They rifle through the blankets for the dry kernels. They are hungry, always hungry. There were eight teats and nine of them. All born live, they all survived. The nursing, sleeping and waking, the available, well-milked mother are all distant memories. But the hunger, the drive, the life-and-death pursuit of food remains strongly implanted. Now they are plumping, growing and gaining. They are entering nine weeks. Their poop is well-formed and abundant. They must be fortified, well fed, and fine tuned for the adopting, the departing, the transitioning. They will need some excess, some margin, some grace. The new homes will not do it perfectly the first few nights and days. There will be new vet introductions, second and third vaccinations, kid over-petting and palming. There will be new toys, neighborhood and relatives' adornment and adoration. And there will be missing and longing for the collective heartbeat of the siblings, the warm pile of the slumbering, the rousting and rising, the clock driven routine of the kennel, the pack's rising and falling rhythm without them.

Not Without Hope

One by one each dog slipped through my grasp, my responsibility, my control, into the realm of beyond my help. Some were old, truly old, with debilitating diseases that damage organs or become bleeds. I trusted my beloved veterinarian with all his seen-it-before wisdom and good sense to guide me step by step. We tried, the two of us together, to first do no harm, then manage resulting symptoms even if we couldn't beat the underlying disease. My success, hope, and state of mind were intertwined with his expertise more than he could ever know. His street-smart approach often translated into a dog's quality of life for weeks, months or in some cases years.

One pleasant ordinary June day, I finish morning chores by noon and spend the next few hours in the house otherwise occupied. At 4 o'clock I begin evening rounds as I always do. Stepping into the fenced compound I notice erratic movement in one of the corner pens closest to the gate. I am horrified to see our 10 year old female Lily scooting around on the concrete. Her front legs dragging her rag doll rear around her little six foot enclosure. Her male companion River is springing up on their flat-topped dog house knowing it's time for evening let outs. Lily normally joins him in this self rising and lowering via a couple of concrete steps. It is their old-age version of pacing in a small space. I open their pen immediately. River bounds out into the play yard as he always does. Lily makes the effort but needs me to help her to all fours. She sways, crossing over her back legs in an extreme drunken-sailor stagger before falling over. I know this is a very bad sign because of the severe loss of movement and the sudden onset. She was fine just a few short hours ago.

In the time it takes to load her, grab keys, purse, call in, and drive to my vet, Lily has gone from poor rear movement to no rear movement. Even when a hemostat is clamped on a toe to test her reaction to pain, my sweet dog has no response, feels nothing, doesn't move to pull her leg away. She is admitted to the hospital with hopes resting on intravenous steroids, antibiotics and some expensive wonder drug called DMSO.

Forty-eight hours later I get the follow-up veterinarian call reporting Lily is paralyzed in all four legs. My heart sinks. With the phone still to my ear I hear him saying "You might want to take her home, give her a few days... she'll be off IV but you could continue oral steroids... at least through the weekend... see if she improves at all. We are done with the DMSO treatment which had to be given intravenously."

I see my future self carrying her around for days, washing pee and poop from her beautiful white coat, I see myself struggling to get her to eat, propping her up with blankets, positioning her so she is upright, so she doesn't choke.

"I have to be honest," he continues, "The longer she is paralyzed, the less chance she has of ever recovering... but you might want to give her a few more days. Most folks aren't set up to managing it, but I think you'll be okay."

I see my future self loading a still paralyzed dog back into the car weeks later, after nights and days crying over *how long was long enough? How could I kill anything because her care was too much work? How could I let her live on completely paralyzed?*

In my silence he continues, "We would normally keep her here for four days, she's been here for two... You are already at $900... $1500 if we keep her till Friday. But it's up to you. I understand if you don't want to try."

I want to be brave enough to give him permission to put her down right now. *Would I go in and be with her when they did it? Or just once could I be spared?*

Reading my silent thoughts he adds, "She is old but it's not without hope."

On automatic pilot now, I tell him I will come to get her. I'll keep her through the weekend. At least that way I can say goodbye.

Once I am bench seated in examination room number three, two vet techs carry flat-out Lily by stretcher, setting her down to the floor. She lifts her head when she sees me. Her eyes and mouth grin happy I am there. I kneel over her. Bending forward I put my face to hers. She licks my lips and tears. There was no preparing myself for how paralyzed was paralyzed... she could not move anything at all but her head. Now my vet is in the room explaining her bowels and bladder will be involuntary. She will need to be kept clean, moved out of it, propped up to eat and drink. Rolled over to her other side every two hours. Limbs should be massaged and manipulated to mimic normal movement. I should orally continue her high doses of Prednisone.

As the techs slide her from the stretcher to the folded down backseat area of my vehicle, my vet says, "Look very closely for any sign of leg movement, even an inch or less... watch for it. Let us know."

On the drive home, she looks like a small bearskin white rug. I tilt my rear view mirror to her image. It is not looking good but I remind myself that he has said "It's not without hope." On the drive, I think about every possible way I can keep her clean and comfortable. I've set up a very large crate on our back porch, building up the crate tray with several metal grids to create a gap under the dog, an adult version of a puppy exercise pen. I'm hoping that pee will run under the dog into the tray without her laying in it. I've folded a small blanket for padding on top of that so she might lay comfortably with her back defecating end just off the edge. I rolled up towels to create a soft border at all edges. I want to make sure her lifeless feet do not get caught in the crate. We could unintentionally injure her further. She will wear a suitcase harness so she has handles whenever we need to maneuver her.

A large plastic bin located beside the crate is loaded up with towels, blankets and cleanup solution. Additional garbage bags, newspapers and laundry baskets just about fill the tiny porch. I am grateful it is warm weather. She can stay in a bug-free screened porch and have an outside place near a hose. Better cleaning for messes than inside our house. The sliding door from my dining kitchen allows me to check on her without disturbing. Best yet she is only about 30 feet from the kennel enclosure so she can see and hear the other dogs. This is the safest way I can continue her normal life.

Now home, I park very near the porch. I lift her head and chest, slipping the harness under and around her. She is heavy deadweight. I sling her down from the tailgate to the grass. It feels odd to leave her laying there unleashed, while I prop open the screen door and crate, even though I know she can't run off. The rest of the dogs are barking and watching from their fencing. This is not the Lily they know. I lug her into the porch and slide her into the crate back end first remembering to put her on the opposite side from the ride home. I fuss with propping her head until I think she is comfortable.

The two-hour break 'til rolling her onto her back to her other side is short. Every rollover, I massage her limbs, folding and bending them, mimicking walking movement. I squeeze each foot. I prop her up so she lays on her belly when I hold a water bowl to her or force pills down her throat. I am grateful she is willing to eat and drink. It isn't until the next day that I see urine in the tray of the crate. I am relieved to know she can pee. At least her bladder still works.

My husband, home on the weekend, makes it his task to take her out of the crate every two hours. He remembers which new side to lay her on when he slides her butt back into its porch cell. He insists she still needs to get out like a normal dog. He pulls her out carefully. He carries her down four wooden steps. Holding her up by harness he moves her along as if they are walking together. Her four legs drag behind her. I take the opportunity of these outings to empty and rinse the crate tray. I remove any soiled bedding. I reset blankets and towels. From the porch I see my husband now at our yard's woodsy edge holding Lily up by harness with one hand while manipulating range of motion for each leg with the other. He sets each foot down in its proper flexed position instead of its paralyzed rolling-backward state. I am not strong enough to execute this physical therapy even if I had thought of it. But he is. So he does.

After seeing her legs dangling I don't think she has a rat's chance come high water, but I admire his sweet efforts. Sometimes not knowing what you are up against is better. A little blind-faith believing can be helpful too.

By the next day we realize she is holding pee while in the crate and releasing it when she is out on her virtual walks! At first I thought I was wishful thinking when from the corner of my eye I detected a slight motion of one leg. I remembered my vet saying look very closely. Later, while positioning her bedding behind her, I do see a twitch. First one foot then the other. Next she seems to try to squat to pee on her outings. Rear legs still mostly limp but she is able to drop her tail towards the soft grass.

Back in the work week before his early morning shift, my husband takes Lily out fake-walking in the wet grass. She pees and poops after a long still night. She is too heavy for me, but I struggle her out several times during the day. He rushes home after work and takes over until bedtime. Little by little Lily is starting to take some of her own weight. Legs are dragging less. I am thrilled to let my vet know we are making progress. We pay and transport Lily three times per week for acupuncture treatments he thinks might complement the therapy we are doing.

In several weeks all motion returns to Lily. She is a stately whole functioning dog. We maintain her separate porch quarters and continue leash walking a bit longer before cautiously returning her to her place in our kennel.

As I write this today, she is alive and well with full mobility. She is sixteen years old. We experienced at least one miracle.

About Cowboy

He is one of my biggest males at sixty pounds of, I hate to think it, almost deadweight. At fourteen years old, his age somewhat softens the blow but doesn't make him any lighter. Now my back and knee really feel discomfort in the task of making him more comfortable. "I love you. Good boy" I offer him a little drink from a stainless steel bowl. A few laps comfort me. Hopefully he'll go back to sleep now. I rub the soft, coarse fur. He is fragrant and clean from the earlier bath and his thick coat is mostly dry. He is a nearly reliable alarm clock, calling at a predictable 3 am each morning. That is how long he can hold his evening fluids. I imagine he gets stiff and needs to move or in his case, be moved by then.

It is no easy task, being summoned from a dream state, called into service for something that most dogs can perform for themselves. Lots of old ones have come and gone before with their ancient wisdom, moon-faced, full ruff, regal thick coats and chiseled arctic heads, each with their own eventual trouble.

This once agile male has a very unique coat patterning called piebald. His bright white face spreads to the back of his head, neck and shoulders forming a lovely white shawl against his dark red coat. Some other white irregular shapes on his back and croup remind of a Pinto or Holstein and encouraged me to name him Cowboy. His forward-driving trot and blue eyes he inherited from his copper-coated father who was my first American/Canadian Champion. He passed these same traits onto his handsome son.

Cowboy can still walk short distances without help. He can still sniff where the girl dogs have peed. He can rub his head or face into my hand or his soft blankets, grateful for the rub or scratch. He can still pee and poop with some assistance. His urinating squat sometimes gets too low and getting back up to stand becomes difficult. Momentum helps him trot down the hill of the long driveway out to the fresh front yard grass, but standing up on his own has become impossible. He just doesn't have the back and strength to rise to all fours.

At dawn I move this magnificent dog to his outdoor day pen to be with old girl Fleur de Lily. They sleep curled, back touching back in two opposing crescents. They nap peacefully for several hours waking mid-morning with yawns and big stretches. She scolds him if he sniffs her romantically or he gazes at her uneaten food.

It has been many happy weeks since the night it first crossed my mind that it might be time to take him. It has been cool, not humid and the flies and mosquitoes have not been bad. When he woofs for assistance or relief, I have promptly attended to him.

I am uniquely available and qualified to do so. I have helped him rise so he could stride down the hill of the driveway, finally unleashed, front paws crossing, but moving gently, steadily forward, to the front yard to lay in the cool green thickness and eat or nuzzle tender blades of grass. He sleeps in the cool air conditioning of the downstairs. A few times he has slept through the whole night. A small wound on the side of his forehead, maybe from a stumble, became infected under the dark fur and I cleaned it by repeated wiping with surgical gauze and Nolvasan. It healed up leaving a little bald scar.

They all had rough patches, like old humans. Restless days or nights when I would wonder should this be the last. Then they would rally many, many times to good meals, good weather and a peaceful breeze.

Today Cowboy is serene and pain free. There is no absurd human talk or thoughts of dying with dignity. I know dogs want to live in the moment of every day. Today I have him and will not weep. I will care for him and any of my dogs fiercely. I will wage the war on pee loving maggots, offer treats for loss of appetite, launder bedding for aging hygiene, dread fatiguing immobility and all other old dog trouble. I will not think about the final moments and the euthanasia IV line. My back and knee will take it another day.

The Number

I hate the question. That is why I answer something else.

"He's thirteen years old," I say about my Siberian Husky boy
Domino.

"Yeah," says the other, "I noticed he's limping."

"A bit of arthritis, but my vet thinks he gets on well for a dog of
his age."

"Awe, that's good" she says, reassured by my vet's opinion.

Domino comes over to me then, looking up admiringly. His
dark brown eyes are framed by white eyelashes. His shaggy coat
sports diamond shapes; white against the faded black creates a small
shawl at his shoulders. "What can I do with such a sweet old boy?" I
say scratching behind his ears. Domino rubs his neck deeply into my
hands and presses his side along my thigh as he trots off. I catch the
eye of the older man of the group. He smiles at me.

Four of them, plastic cups in hand, have wandered over from the
neighbor's double wide and are standing at the edge of my
woods gaping at the dogs in the exercise yard. Whenever I see these
cup holders approach, I wave them over closer. It is better to be
friendly and let them take a full look, ask their 'poor dog' questions
up front. Be nosy with my cooperation. Some would be genuinely
interested. Others were what I called the *fix its*, I had one dog once
so I know all about it folks.

I started dog chores earlier than usual this morning. It is the best way to have my dogs settled and quiet so as not to disturb their party. I did an extra thorough job of scrubbing and scooping, not wanting to offend when typically a few of their guests do wander over. We had gotten an invitation, and dropped by earlier with a cashed- up graduation card. We want to be neighborly, give the kid a gift, smooth any feathers our dogs might have ruffled, and get out.

I wander close to the fence while carrying a hoe and dustpan with its long stand-up handle. I continue to be chatty with the spectators while getting any missed poop from the dog yard. I notice some of the stools are mushy because of the early rain. I want to pick it all up before it rains again this evening as is forecast. Our tall treed woods with its shady dirt floor makes it difficult to find every brown on brown.

I am the resident poopologist. I can tell by the size and shape which belongs to which dog. I am always looking to evaluate the consistency. If a dog is eating too much it might be a little unformed. Roundworms common to canines might show up. Stool can be a diagnostic tool for older dogs too. Black or tarry can indicate stomach or intestinal bleeding. Liquid or foul-smelling can be a sign of sickness.

A small crowd is gathering now. The persistent woman asks the dreaded question again. I try a vague answer on her, the one I've requested my husband reply when he is in the same position. "Well, we have a few retired teams and then we have our younger up-and-coming group."

I figure the questioner can do their own approximate math then, couple old teams, couple young teams. That should be good enough... from their vantage point they can see the groups of penned dogs to the side and back so they'll have some idea.

Yeah, sure I thought, we do have a lot of dogs. As my husband is approaching retirement, we had the end-of-dog discussion again. Were we ready to let all the old dogs die off and when the last was gone we were done? Or were we going to keep a few young ones so we could continue to enjoy breeding, showing and dog sledding? I was not ready to quit. I started my breeding program with some excellent genetics that others had carefully brought forth. I had continued it for six generations over the past 30 years. I could not give that up.

"Yeah but how many? I mean total?"

Okay, here we go. The bold, the few, the persistent, there was one in every crowd. Probably had a few other beers before she brought over a full plastic cup, now empty.

At my age my goal IS to keep fewer, even better quality whose genetics included many of my older worthy stock. I am being selective, strictly evaluating type, health, longevity, temperament, as I've seen some mentors do before me. The quality of pups I am having now is amazing.

I say, "What you may not realize is I have many older ones."

She continues on, "You mean if one of us wanted to buy one of these adult dogs you wouldn't sell it?"

" We do have some young adults available for adoption."

"You wouldn't sell an older one? What about him?" She gestures towards Domino.

She had no idea Domino had girlfriends and kids, his routine. This was his place of birth and it would be his place of death. He loved the life he'd known. Having many dogs was a lot of work especially if you were maintaining and supporting the old ones, while bringing forth the new. The economics of the whole package is grinding. No amount of dog food sales, puppies, boarding, grooming or sled presentations can even begin to offset the growing cost of doing the right thing.

"As a breeder it's really valuable to know how their life and health plays out. We believe in a golden retirement for those who have served us so well. It's the most labor intensive, expensive way to do it, but we feel it is the right thing to do."

The spectating group is about fifteen now. Some are nodding, "Yes, that is good." They were starting to get it.

The persistent women asks again. "So how many DO you have. Do you know?"

I could revert to my classic answers; *A lot. Too many* or *more than you could handle* or lay my original joke on her: *It's not polite to ask a woman's age or the number of dogs she has*, then I'd add, *but in my case it is about the same number*. That last one would make her eyes wide. Turn her thoughts inward. I'd see them all figuring in their heads knowing I was not a young women! Yikes!

The Number, the number, the number. The constant pressure to let go of the dogs, cut back on the number. People who cared for me, strangers I'd never met, having no idea of the genetics, the attachment, the investment, sure they knew best, better than me. What number is okay? How about 10 or 22 or 38 or 55? What number is too many?

I know a breeder with only three dogs, all females. Everyone is bred every heat or at least every year and sometimes twice in a year for her entire fertile life from her first heat till at least 10 years old. One of his bitches had 11 litters, not counting the still births in between. He considered her of such high quality, he said it was his duty to the breed to breed her. His dogs, even at middle age looked dragged, drooped and completely ragged out, but you'd love his answer, he just has three.

"What is it about knowing the number?" I look directly at her this time. "Isn't the real question how well are they loved and cared for?"

"We had an old dog once." She shakes her head. "I cried for weeks after. I miss him so much I could never have a dog again."

Staring at her welling tears, I hate the question because they are not just a number to me either. They are the son of the son of my fairest daughter, they are the coming up youngsters with potential to fulfill, they are the matriarch or patriarchs that have led my team with their siblings and offspring, now retired or deceased. They are the stillborn puppy who had been revived and hand fed, who made it, still happily squawking at her 12 year old Uncle who adores her. He licks her feet and ears daily while she bosses the bed they shared. She was having the happiest time. I couldn't imagine my group of dogs without her.

There has been much bad press about over-breeding and big numbers of animals discovered and rescued. "Puppies are cash crops to some farmers" was the name of an informative article I read early on. It is good to support the folks that are doing it right, avoid those who are taking advantage and abusing their animals. See facilities. Meet dog parents and grandparents. Observe the level of care, check references including calling the breeder's veterinarian. It is good to cast a light on hoarders, puppy millers, pet stores and backyard breeders. The rest of us who have humbly given our lives to it to the point of exhaustion, bankruptcy, foolishness and trauma think it has gone a little overboard. My dogs are happy, well fed and cared for, even though it is taking its toll on me.

Her husband pipes up now. "My father was a farmer. He said it best. If you have livestock at some point it will be dead stock... Ever think of that?"

After 30 plus years and six generations. Really? You think I haven't looked death in its inevitable face, fought it back for weeks or months? Think I haven't gone to great lengths to save old dogs many, many times? Think I haven't taken dogs for their last happy ride and ended up at my vet's, giving them hundreds of dollars to spare a beloved friend his final miserable hours, knowing that some disease is about to get really steep and steal the last ounce of quality life the dog has left? Think I haven't bathed an old one everyday till his skin is raw and sore, having crapped himself for the 110th time? You think I haven't wiped up released bowel and pee from the floor or my brow? Think I haven't been at his side when one of my most beloved howled his pack song with his last breath while I stroked his soft white fur?

"Live stock, dead stock, Yeah, I know."

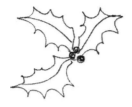

Reasons

The steady groan of the gristmill grinding, the rise and bend of migrants tending onions in the blackened earth, and the faithful touching the worn toe of the marble virgin have their reasons. I have my reasons too, 50 of them in black, red or gray, trimmed with white faces and feet. Their upright fur bristles soft. Amber or blue eyes flash light. Each fox brush tail flags Siberian Husky exuberance. They are a pack, my pack, but there is much more to it than admiration.

In just-light morning, I pull a stiff coverall over soft sweats. I squeeze into used boots remembering I need the gate key in my pocket. I slip out into pine-scrubbed air, welcome a brightening sky, and follow a footpath to their fenced building. I find the jagged slot for the small key and slip it into the hanging padlock. I secure the chain link gate behind me and open the door to the warming room. The walls are flanked with storage cabinets and metal food cans as well as a cast iron claw-foot bathtub mounted at counter height. The concrete floor is polished smooth and rubber door mats guard the slippery entryway.

A utility cart is prominently parked. Last year's only Christmas list item, it greets me each new day. With its tall-edged tray, sturdy push handle, and indentations for small items, it is the perfect assistant. I've topped it with stacks of stainless bowls, a dry kibble pail, measuring scoop, and worn but clean towels. An empty Maxwell House blue plastic coffee container is repurposed as a pitcher. On the lower tier a thin pipe sticks out of a bucket of water. I use it for dumping stainless pails through chain link without reentering each kennel. A Tupperware bin of wood shavings is placed for easy scattering over urine or adding fresh bedding to doghouses.

This polypropylene tank of a cart with its caster swivel wheels stands ready for hours of feeding, scooping, and scrubbing. Even with its help, I'm chapped, chafed, scraped, and strained. I order, receive, pay for, store, and transport 40 pound bags of feed and bales of shavings. It can't assist me with brutally cold metal pen latches difficult to manipulate while wearing gloves. It can't make water freeze less quickly, or scoop and store poop in plastic buckets and dispose of it daily. But it's by my side when every morning's high hopes to press on, get it done, are whisked away by afternoon wind when labor drags on.

The dogs stir quietly as I enter. Some don't roust much. Across the room through another door, I walk the 120-foot hallway to check on each of the twenty pens. Every few dogs have a six-foot housing area with floor space, dog houses and a dog door to an outside run. I enter a few of the gated kennels with a poop scoop. Some dogs defecate inside instead of going out the dog door as I prefer. It's cold out there this morning. I shouldn't blame them for wanting to eliminate indoors. I check thermometers and adjust thermostats. I take inventory. *Does everyone seem well?* I look at water pails. *Are they empty or frozen? Do they have a thin layer of ice recently formed that will break easily with my pipe?* Some minus-zero mornings the steel buckets don't quite rise above freezing even with heaters on. *Will they need thawing and refilling? Will toping with hot be enough?*

When I return to the warming room the dogs become more active. They hear water filling the pail. They hear the clinking sounds of the dry food in stainless bowls.
As I progress setting up the feed, their pacing and whining increases. The vocalizing is anticipating the feeding. My presence is incidental.

I fill each bowl with two and a half cups of dry kibble. I make five, ten bowl stacks, counting as I go. The dog clamor increases as I begin to add warm water from a blue coffee scoop to each. They know I am minutes away from serving it to each of them in their kennel runs. I open and distribute a can of food for a few picky eaters. I hide medication for a few elders too. Now ready, the cart is an organized clutter of filled bowl stacks, extra water, a metal food bucket, a can opener, utensils, and containers of special treats. Doctored bowls are in separate corners so I can keep track of who gets each. The cart is loaded heavy but can bump up over the door jam out of the warm room and into the cool hallway. I am careful not to stack to tipping heights.

The main event starts as soon as the cart is in the walkway. I work to focus on each specific task while group mentality is erupting into deafening noise. Delivering correct food, and in some cases meds, is a must. Specific care by tending to each individuals needs. Every dog is yelling, leaping, dancing, screaming as they wait for the serving station to roll their way. My goal is to move along slow enough to watch several pens devour, but fast enough to appease the frantic waiting masses.

I deliver a warm bowl of food to each dog. I start at the closest pen. I set a meal in front of each, as far apart from each other as the pen's arrangement will allow. The dogs dive in. I'm careful each animal does not spill it as I set it down. I have trained them to stay in their own bowl, not take another's which could cause a fight. Some obey. Some swap half-eaten bowls every day agreeing between themselves. Most are paired, mother and offspring, or two siblings that have their *we've always done it this way* plan. One pair of sisters guard and growl, but eat all and never fight. Another fussy pest leaves the bottom bits and I remove it or she'll stand by it all day. As long as all comply without squabbling I allow.

I am as loud as they are some days in the worst behaved pens, shouting *no jumping*, stomping my feet or banging empty bowls if two dogs standoff over a few spilled crumbs. I am sweet and encouraging to a few meeker dogs. I gesture towards others to leap on top of flat houses to take their meal above while others eat below. It is a wild noisy time. My sprung nerves are on edge as I wheel my way 120 feet. Big responsibility in mostly controlled chaos, my heart and temper in my mouth, I will do anything in these moments to make it go well.

I inch my way one pen at a time. Caring for each creature in their moment. The volume decreases. More have eaten than are still waiting to eat. The last few pens are individual speak instead of mass song. I set the last two bowls to a once mated pair, her feed set inside her doghouse, her mate's set alongside it. She eats faster and tries to steal. I linger a few moments to make sure he gets it all before she approaches.

Emptier now, I roll the cart back towards the warming room as I collect empty bowls. I tend to each hanging water pail. I confirm each dog ate all that was given. I admire each little family group. I notice body language. *Are they content? Did their meal land well? Did any animosity arise between bunk mates?*

I treasure the peaceful moment. Fed dogs are licking bowls, sniffing out any spilled crumbs. Some have pushed empty bowls under chain-link rails into the walkway where I easily collect them. Some have already bedded back down. Some have gone outdoors for dog business or to greet me when I scoop their outside runs. Then they will nap until I make my next rounds. It is a few short hours before I am back for more watering or to snack or scoop them or to give the evening meal. The dogs are wanting, always wanting. They are demanding, enchanting beauties and there are 50 of them. They are grandparents, mothers, fathers, sons and daughters. They are Champions and misfits. They are dying elders and bounding youth.

It has been a 30-year, six-generation obsession really, but it feels just like love.

No Place Like Home

Arctic dogs of agile eye,

tufting fur, elated tribe,

my gravity, my compass,

my connection to the earth.

There is no time for much else,

a few scraps on a napkin,

a portrait-owed client.

Listing tasks unending.

Swaying trees black

in desolate beauty.

Winter light now moving

canvas of my youth.

My birth, my death, my toil

circle season. Place

of blue and white cold.

Many dogs flash.

I am home.

Made in the USA
Middletown, DE
01 February 2018